Persuasion Power

Mastering Essential Communication Techniques

Table of Contents

1. Introduction 1

2. Unlocking the Key to Effective Communication 2

    2.1. The Basics of Effective Communication 2

    2.2. Honing Active Listening Skills 3

    2.3. The Power of Non-verbal Communication 3

    2.4. The Art of Persuasion 4

    2.5. Conflict Management 4

    2.6. The Power of Positive Communication 5

3. Understanding Five Core Techniques of Persuasion 6

    3.1. Rapport Building: Connecting on a Personal Level 6

    3.2. The Art of Storytelling: Triggering Engagement and
Empathy 7

    3.3. Effective Listening: Absorb and Understand 7

    3.4. Constructive Questioning: Invoking Thought and Dialogue ... 8

    3.5. Emotional Appeal: Invoking Sentiments 9

4. Charm: Your Invisible Weapon of Influence 10

    4.1. Understanding Charm 10

    4.2. Cultivating Charm 10

    4.3. Charm in Professional Settings 11

    4.4. Charm in Person-to-Person Interactions 12

    4.5. The Artistic Button of Charm 12

    4.6. The Road to Personal Growth 13

5. The Subtle Art of Non-Verbal Communication 14

    5.1. Understanding Non-Verbal Signals 14

    5.2. Body Language 14

    5.3. Eye Contact 15

    5.4. Space and Touch 15

    5.5. Voice 15

5.6. Non-Verbal Communication across Cultures 16

5.7. Non-verbal Self-Check 16

6. Active Listening: A Cornerstone of Persuasion 17

6.1. The Concept of Active Listening 17

6.2. The Process of Active Listening 17

6.3. Active Listening and Its Influence on Persuasion 18

6.4. Practical Techniques to Enhance Active Listening 19

7. Leveraging Emotional Intelligence for Successful Negotiation . . . 20

7.1. The Pillars of Emotional Intelligence 20

7.2. Harnessing Self-Awareness and Self-Regulation 21

7.3. Empathy: The Heart of Successful Negotiation 21

7.4. Motivation and Negotiation 22

7.5. Applying Social Skills in Negotiation 22

7.6. Conclusion 22

8. Crafting and Delivering Compelling Messages 24

8.1. Understanding the Art of Crafting Messages 24

8.2. The Power of Storytelling 25

8.3. Framework for Delivering Compelling Messages 25

8.4. The Power of Repetition 26

9. Overcoming Communication Barriers and Misunderstandings . . 27

9.1. Types of Communication Barriers 27

9.1.1. Physical Barriers 27

9.1.2. Psychological Barriers 28

9.1.3. Semantic Barriers 28

9.1.4. Process Barriers 28

9.2. Overcoming Misunderstandings 28

9.2.1. Seek Clarity 28

9.2.2. Give and Request Feedback 29

9.2.3. Practice Active Listening 29

9.3. Enhancing Your Communication Skills 29

9.3.1. Articulation and Clarity 29

9.3.2. Non-Verbal Cues 29

9.3.3. Empathy in Communication 29

9.3.4. Cultural Competency 30

10. Mastering the Power of Persuasion in Leadership 31

10.1. Understanding Persuasion 31

10.2. Constructing a Persuasive Argument 32

10.3. Emotional Intelligence and Persuasion 33

10.4. Framing and Reframing: The Power of Perception 33

10.5. Storytelling in Persuasive Leadership 34

11. Harnessing Persuasion Power: Real-World Applications 35

11.1. Understanding Persuasion and Power 35

11.2. Negotiation Strategies: Power Moves 36

12. Storytelling: An Ingenious Tool 37

12.1. The Power of Non-Verbal Communication 37

12.2. Persuasion Ethics: The Line of Power 38

Chapter 1. Introduction

Unlock the full potency of your interpersonal communication with our exclusive Special Report titled "Persuasion Power: Mastering Essential Communication Techniques." This easy-to-understand guide is a key to unravel the mystic art of effective persuasion, helping you make a significant transformation in the way you network, negotiate, lead, and influence. Whether it's tilting a business deal in your favor, inspiring your team towards a unified goal, or simply making everyday interactions more meaningful - our special report serves as your personal handbook. At the end of an enjoyable read, you are not just purchasing a report, but investing in a life altering skill of mastering the art of communication!

Chapter 2. Unlocking the Key to Effective Communication

Effective communication is not just about speaking, but understanding the essence of transmission of thoughts and ideas. Your ability to persuade others, influence decisions, conquer disagreements, and manage conflicts often depends on how well you communicate. In this inclusive guide, you will comprehend the keys to unlocking effective interpersonal communication.

2.1. The Basics of Effective Communication

Let's start with the basics. Communication involves the transfer of information from one source to another. This information could be conveyed orally, through body language, or written text. But, what makes communication **effective** is not just the clear transmission of this information. It's also about ensuring the intended message is received accurately, fostering understanding, and propelling actions to favorable outcomes.

The main components defining communication are:

1. Sender: This is the source of the communication or the person with the information to share.

2. Message: This is the information the sender wishes to transmit.

3. Channel: This is the medium used by the sender to communicate the message.

4. Receiver: This is the individual or group the sender is trying to communicate with.

5. Feedback: This refers to the receiver's response to the sender's

message, indicating that the message was received and understood (or not).

The blockers to effective communication could be anything from noise (literal or metaphorical), cultural differences, language barriers, emotional biases, or simply a lack of interest.

2.2. Honing Active Listening Skills

Active listening is a significant part of effective communication. Truly listening to someone means focusing not just on the words, but also the feelings, the subtexts, and the unsaid messages.

Tips to active listening:

1. Maintain eye contact.

2. Show that you are interested and involved.

3. Provide feedback to show understanding- summarizing, paraphrasing etc.

4. Avoid interrupting the speaker.

5. Ask open-ended questions for clarity.

Compared to a plain listener, an active listener reaps stronger connections, improved understanding, and enhanced trust, making active listening a powerful tool of communication.

2.3. The Power of Non-verbal Communication

A considerable chunk of our communication is non-verbal, and it's essential to understand the impact of body language, facial expressions, gestures, and even tone of voice. Non-verbal cues often affect the meaning of our words and are powerful tools for persuasion.

Some tips to effectively use non-verbal communication:

1. Maintain an open and neutral body posture.

2. Match your facial expressions with your sentiments.

3. Keep a light and friendly tone.

Non-verbal communication becomes even more important when dealing with people from diverse cultures where language might itself be a barrier.

2.4. The Art of Persuasion

Persuasion is a key element of effective communication. It involves convincing others with your point of view and influencing their choices.

Here are some steps to be effective at persuasion:

1. Understand your audience: Tailor your argument to match their values and viewpoints.

2. Use solid facts and logical reasoning: People are more likely to be persuaded if your arguments are backed by facts.

3. Show enthusiasm: People often judge the merit of something by the passion backing it.

2.5. Conflict Management

Effective communication is an essential tool in conflict management. The ability to express and decipher the emotions effectively plays an important role in resolving disputes.

Tips for using communication in conflict management:

1. Emphasize calm, clear speaking and listening.

2. Encourage shared problem-solving.

3. Encourage expressing respective feelings.

2.6. The Power of Positive Communication

Effective communication is also about delivering and receiving messages positively. Positive communication builds healthier relationships, boosts morale, and increases satisfaction.

Tips for positive communication:

1. Provide constructive feedback.

2. Show appreciation for good contributions.

3. Avoid blame games and approach situations constructively.

In conclusion, effective communication is a multifaceted skill involving listening, non-verbal signals, persuasion, conflict management, and positive communication. By understanding and applying these principles, you can significantly enhance your interpersonal skill set, leading to improved relationships both personally and professionally.

Chapter 3. Understanding Five Core Techniques of Persuasion

The art of persuasion is nuanced and dynamic, encompassing vital realms of communication. In this pursuit, we present to you five core techniques that are the cornerstone of excellence in persuasion. They include Rapport Building, The Art of Storytelling, Effective Listening, Constructive Questioning, and Emotional Appealing.

3.1. Rapport Building: Connecting on a Personal Level

At the grassroots level, the power of persuasion is born out of relationships. Rapport building is the foremost step in creating a firm foundation for persuasion. It involves finding commonalities, embracing differences, and fostering genuine interest and empathy in your interactions.

Rapport can be established through different avenues:

1. The mirroring technique: Here, we mimic the speech, body language, or other behavioral aspects of the person we're conversing with. This induces a sense of familiarity, leading to increased comfort and rapport.

2. Genuine Interest: Invest time and effort to know the individual on a personal level. Understand their interests, hobbies, and values. This will also make you more equipped to communicate in a manner that resonates with them.

3. Active Empathy: Actively try to understand and share the feelings of others. Genuine empathy promotes a deeper connection and

instills trust.

3.2. The Art of Storytelling: Triggering Engagement and Empathy

Telling a story is not just about relating facts. It's about weaving connections and invoking emotions. Stories foster connections and allow individuals to perceive experiences and scenarios through your perspective. A well-narrated story can stimulate emotions, imprint memorable images, and bolster your persuasive power.

To master the art of narrative persuasion, there are certain elements to consider:

1. The Hook: Your story should have an exciting and engaging beginning to capture the listener's attention.

2. The Journey: This part is where you delve into the details, engage with your emotional content, and propagate the primary notion of your story.

3. The Moral: End with a convincing or impactful note, providing a clear message or conclusion.

3.3. Effective Listening: Absorb and Understand

Effective listening is a pillar of good communication and persuasion. It involves not just hearing the spoken words but understanding the emotions, intentions, and subtle cues lying underneath. It's about showing genuine interest in the speaker's views, asking relevant questions, and providing thoughtful responses.

Here are a few tips to improve your listening skills:

1. Stay Focused: Avoid getting distracted and keep your attention steadfast on the speaker.

2. Reflective Listening: Repeat or paraphrase the speaker's statements in your own words to confirm the accurate comprehension of their point.

3. Non-Verbal Signs: Pay heed to the unspoken language of the speaker, including facial expressions, gesture, and posture to get a complete sense of their message.

3.4. Constructive Questioning: Invoking Thought and Dialogue

Questions can be potent tools in persuasion, helping in creating a two-way interaction, propagating curiosity, fostering dialogue, and bridging gaps in understanding.

To use questions effectively:

1. Open-Ended Questions: Use questions that require more than a 'yes' or 'no' answer, forcing the respondent to think and provide detailed answers.

2. Thought-Provoking Questions: Ask questions that incite deep thought and self-reflection, leading to greater self-awareness and impetus for change.

3. Follow Up Questions: Clarifying and confirming responses drive the conversation deeper and demonstrate your interest and active engagement.

3.5. Emotional Appeal: Invoking Sentiments

Human beings, though rational, are immensely driven by their emotions. Emotionally charged communication can deeply influence attitudes and trigger action. Appeal to emotions like joy, fear, pride, or altruism to enhance your persuasive game.

To tap into emotional appeal:

1. Evoke Positive Emotions: Associating your argument or proposition to positive emotions, like joy or satisfaction, can make it more appealing.

2. Use Appropriate Emotional Language: Using words that invoke emotion can strengthen your argument and draw in your listeners.

3. Appeal to Moral Values: Aligning your message with a person's moral values can appeal to their emotions effectively.

Each technique holds a unique power in influencing, persuading, and driving change. Harnessing these techniques will help you customize your communication approach, making it more appealing to your audience, and significantly enhancing your persuasive power. Nevertheless, remember that genuine intentions and empathy form the baseline of all persuasive interactions.

Chapter 4. Charm: Your Invisible Weapon of Influence

Your charm can be your secret weapon, an invisible force that sways hearts and minds, opening a world of opportunities for you. The ability to charm is less about superficial attractiveness and more about the power to make others feel good about themselves.

4.1. Understanding Charm

Charm is an irresistible quality that magnetizes others, making them feel important, seen, and appreciated. It's a subtle blend of diplomacy, wit, and genuine interest in others that can open doors and convince people to act in harmony with your objectives.

Being charming is about mood regulation and influencing feelings. It involves creating a positive aura around you that is palpable to those in your presence. This quality is one that often aids in persuasion, as people are more inclined to help those they find charming.

4.2. Cultivating Charm

It's a myth that charm is something you're either born with or not. Anyone can learn and nurture this winning trait. Here are some key strategies:

1. Practice Active Listening: Charming individuals have a knack for making others feel understood. They achieve this by listening actively, demonstrating openness and genuine engagement to what the speaker is saying. By practicing active listening, you can respond appropriately and lead the conversation in a beneficial

direction.

2. Show Genuine Interest: Make a conscious effort to show interest in the other person's ideas, thoughts, and experiences. This makes them feel acknowledged and valued - key components in unlocking your persuasion power.

3. Value Body Language: Your physical demeanor sends an array of non-verbal signals. Aim for open, inviting body language: maintain eye contact, use open gestures, and lean slightly towards the person you're interacting with.

4. Balance Confidence and Humility: Walk the thin line between confidence and humility. Exude an aura of self-assuredness without coming off as arrogant. Humility keeps you grounded and demonstrates that you value others.

4.3. Charm in Professional Settings

Charming persuasive communication fosters collaborative, productive environments and helps to nurture relationships that are both personally and professionally rewarding.

During meetings, a charming professional asks meaningful questions that draw out other people's ideas and perspectives, ensuring everyone feels heard. They personify the magic of mutual respect, which paves a path for smoother negotiations.

In job interviews or client presentations, charm can provide that extra push towards success. This skill allows you to convincingly express your value proposition, highlighting your skills, talents, and potential while making the other party feel equally important.

4.4. Charm in Person-to-Person Interactions

In intimate conversations or social gatherings, charm translates into a positive perception of your character, making you likable and influential. It's this power of charm that sets the stage for lasting relationships and connections.

Remember, adapting your behavior to situations and people isn't manipulation – it's about connecting authentically on shared ground. Being self-aware, focused, and genuinely interested in others are critical components of charm that enable you to empathize and engage with sensitivity and warmth, fostering a sense of rapport and trust.

4.5. The Artistic Button of Charm

Understanding and mastering charm takes time, but it is not an impossible task. With mindful practice, self-reflection, empathy, and patience, it can become a powerful catalyst for positive interactions.

Charm is more than just being likable: it is about initiating positive experiences through your presence, sparking a sense of comfort and assurance, and harnessing the power to influence in subtle yet impactful ways. By cultivating this ability, you're not only reassuring others of your intentions but also paving the way for them to reciprocate that comfort and positivity.

Remember that every conversation is a dance – a game of give-and-take. So, take the lead with grace, mindfulness, kindness, and of course, a touch of charm—your invisible weapon of influence.

4.6. The Road to Personal Growth

Commit to this journey of nurturing your charm. Use it as a tool for self-growth, networking, leading, and influencing. Leverage this captivating quality to craft your personal and professional interactions into enriching experiences, setting you apart as you journey towards becoming a master persuader.

Your path to mastering the art of persuasion begins with understanding yourself, your emotions, and your tendencies. By stepping into others' shoes, anticipating their needs, and responding with empathy and sincerity, you can ensure your influence is positive and beneficial. Charm isn't just about self-benefit; it's an investment in yourself, other people, and the quality of your interactions, paving a route towards a more enriching and fulfilling life.

Charm: Your Invisible Weapon of Influence is beyond the techniques or strategies. It's about creating meaningful connections, fostering mutual respect, and creating environments where everyone feels valued and heard. Use your charm wisely, and the world is your stage!

Chapter 5. The Subtle Art of Non-Verbal Communication

Non-verbal communication might easily be overlooked in the face of its more explicit counterpart, but it quietly holds significant influence over the ways we perceive and interpret messages. It applies to our spoken word's tone, facial expressions, body language, gestures, and even short moments of silence. Essentially, the entirety of body language is a silent orchestra, subtly communicating deep-seated emotions and attitudes without uttering a word.

5.1. Understanding Non-Verbal Signals

The first step to master the art of non-verbal communication involves understanding its components, like body language, eye contact, touch, space, and voice. A slight inclination of the head, a 'well-timed' touch, or even appropriate use of personal space can communicate volumes about your attention, sincerity, and respect towards the other person. Irrespective of what your words say, if your non-verbal signals align with them, they amplify trust, clarity, and rapport. On the contrary, if they contradict, they generate tension, confusion, and mistrust.

5.2. Body Language

Body language forms the bedrock of non-verbal communication, embodying itself in posture, gestures, and facial expressions. Encouraging body language, like maintaining an upright posture, emanates confidence and respect. Conversely, a slouching posture may indicate low self-esteem or lack of interest. Small gestures like nodding, pointing, or a simple hand-on-heart can subtly influence the conversation.

Above everything, your facial expressions are window panes to your mind. A genuine smile or a worried frown can often provide more insight into your state than a thousand words. Maintaining relative control over your facial expressions is essential to avoid revealing unintended emotions or thoughts.

5.3. Eye Contact

Eye contact forms the linchpin of effective communication, conveying sincerity, respect, and attention. A consistent eye-contact with occasional breaks indicates an active interest in the conversation and leaves a profound impact. However, steely or prolonged eye-contact can make the other person uncomfortable; as always, the key lies in balance.

5.4. Space and Touch

While often marginalized, the concepts of space and touch hold a unique position in non-verbal communication. Using space wisely, like leaning in during a private conversation or taking a step back during a conflict, can foster comfort and understanding. Similarly, a pat on the back or a hearty handshake can fortify bonds, but intrusion into personal space can led to discomfort and unease.

5.5. Voice

We tend to focus on the words we utter, but 'how' we say them is equally important, including the tone, pitch, speed, and volume of our speech. A calm and steady voice commands respect and trustworthiness, while a high-pitched speedy talk might hint at nervousness or lack of confidence. Understanding the nuances of voice can significantly bolster your persuasive power.

5.6. Non-Verbal Communication across Cultures

Non-verbal cues may vary drastically across cultures, depending on societal norms and traditions. While a firm handshake is seen as a sign of determination in some cultures, it might be considered aggressive in others. Similarly, the interpretation of eye contact, personal space, or gestures can vary widely. To connect meaningfully with people from diverse cultures, it's crucial to respect and comprehend these differences.

5.7. Non-verbal Self-Check

A significant part of non-verbal communication control relates to self-awareness. Acknowledging your non-verbal cues, both consciously and subconsciously exerted, forms the crux of refining your skills. Keeping a check on your own body language, voice, facial expressions, and use of space can enhance the authenticity and impact of your communication.

Non-verbal communication resides beyond the realm of words. It is more about 'how' rather than 'what'. It breathes between our dialogues, quietly imparting more information than we realize. To master this subtle art involves consistently studying, practicing, and refining our actions, which compliments our verbal content with an eloquent symphony of unspoken language. Achieving this harmony is not a destination but a continuous journey, a process of learning and unlearning. But once attained, it offers an invaluable tool of understanding, connecting, and influencing - a potent weapon in our arsenal of persuasive communication.

Chapter 6. Active Listening: A Cornerstone of Persuasion

Listening, in its essence, is not simply a passive activity where you merely act as a receptacle of words. Active listening makes it an engaging process that requires you to fully absorb, comprehend, and respond to the spoken words, fostering a sense of empathy and understanding. This chapter will facilitate a comprehensive understanding of active listening, a cornerstone of persuasive communication.

6.1. The Concept of Active Listening

Active listening involves leaning in, both physically and mentally, to truly understand the speaker's point of view. It includes acknowledging the speaker's feelings and reflecting them, asking questions for clarification, summarizing their statements, and avoiding premature judgement.

The objective of active listening is to develop a deep understanding of the speaker's perspective and feelings. It's about immersing yourself wholeheartedly in their world. This understanding forms the foundation for a persuasive dialogue, as it enables you to tailor your message in a manner that resonates with them.

6.2. The Process of Active Listening

How do we listen actively? Here's a simple, yet effective, four-step process:

1. Focusing: The first step entails fully committing your attention to the speaker. This involves removing distractions and actually investing your time and energy into what the speaker is saying.

2. Comprehending: This is where you make a conscious effort to grasp the speaker's meaning, verbal and non-verbal clues included. Perceive their feelings, thoughts, and ideas.

3. Responding: Active listening is reciprocal. This step includes nodding, maintaining eye contact, and providing feedback such as, "I see," "That's interesting," or "Can you tell me more about that?"

4. Remembering: Remember the main points. This not only shows respect towards the speaker but also aids future conversations, thus helping build rapport and trust.

Practicing these steps will transform your listening skills, making you a better influencer and communicator.

6.3. Active Listening and Its Influence on Persuasion

What role does active listening play in heightening your persuasive powers? The answer to this question lies in the unique capabilities it endows us with:

- Emotional Intelligence: An active listener is in tune with the speaker's emotions, aiding the ability to empathize and respond appropriately. This builds stronger bonds and facilitates the communicator in developing impactful persuasive messages.

- Constructive Feedback: Active listening provides us with deep insights about the speaker's perspective. These insights can be used to frame our arguments or suggestions in a manner that appeals to them.

- Trust and Credibility: By engaging actively in conversations, you show respect and value to the speaker's thoughts. This simple act strengthens trust and elevates your credibility.

In short, active listening turbocharges your persuasive skills, thereby augmenting your overall communication prowess.

6.4. Practical Techniques to Enhance Active Listening

Strengthening your active listening skills isn't an overnight journey. Here are some techniques that provide a guided path towards your target:

- Be Patient: Allow the speaker to communicate their thoughts without interruption.

- Open-ended Queries: Encourage the speaker to elaborate their points by asking questions that can't be answered with a simple 'yes' or 'no'.

- Paraphrase: Restate the speaker's points using your own words. This validates their sentiments and shows that you are fully engaged.

- Non-verbal cues: Pay attention to the speaker's body language. Often, they convey more through gestures than words.

- Silence: Use silence effectively. It gives the speaker time to collect their thoughts and adds value to the conversation.

By consciously embedding these techniques into your routines, you endow yourself with the power of active listening.

This chapter has equipped you with an understanding of active listening and its importance in persuasive communication. By applying this knowledge, moving forward, you can expect to develop stronger connections, build trust, enhance comprehension, and ultimately, elevate your influence.

Chapter 7. Leveraging Emotional Intelligence for Successful Negotiation

Negotiation isn't merely the process of reaching an agreement, but rather a fundamental framework of communication that enables us to ascertain what others want and how we can work together for mutual benefit. This is where Emotional Intelligence (EQ) finds its place. It's about understanding, using, and managing our own emotions in positive ways to relieve stress, communicate effectively, empathize with others, overcome challenges, and defuse conflict.

7.1. The Pillars of Emotional Intelligence

Emotional Intelligence is made up of five key elements, each representing an essential cornerstone in successful negotiation.

1. Self-awareness: This is the ability to recognize your own emotions, strengths, weaknesses, drives, values, and goals, and to understand their impact on others.

2. Self-regulation: It's about managing and regulating your own emotions, especially in stressful situations, to avoid impulsive behaviors or making decisions based on temporary emotions.

3. Motivation: Internal drive to achieve for the sake of achievement. It is a resilient optimism that persists, even in the face of failure.

4. Empathy: This involves noting and understanding the emotions of others, seeing things from their perspective, and making efforts to respond to their emotional reactions.

5. Social skills: These are the skills we use to interact and

communicate with each other, including verbal and non-verbal communication, gestures, body language, and personal appearance.

7.2. Harnessing Self-Awareness and Self-Regulation

Developing self-awareness and self-regulation can significantly improve your performance in negotiations. By becoming aware of your emotional triggers, you can better manage your reaction to tense situations. Being aware enables you to accept the emotions when they occur, without letting them drive your responses.

Self-regulation, on the other hand, is using the awareness to prevent your emotions from hijacking your reasoning. Instead of suppressing emotions, this is about understanding that feelings are temporary and not basing your decisions on transient emotions.

7.3. Empathy: The Heart of Successful Negotiation

A successful negotiator is an empathetic negotiator. Being able to feel what your negotiating partner is experiencing gives you a significant advantage. This doesn't mean being soft, but it means seeking to understand the needs, concerns, and perceptions of your counterpart.

Empathy allows you to predict how others will react, helping you to prepare your arguments and responses efficiently. Emphasizing shared interests can increase the perceived value of the agreement, which will lead to a win-win result.

7.4. Motivation and Negotiation

In negotiations, individuals with high levels of motivation are generally more resilient in the face of failure. They persist and persevere, often devising inventive solutions to seemingly unresolvable disputes.

They are driven to succeed for the sake of achievement rather than external rewards or recognition. Their eagerness to tackle challenges and positive attitude can infectiously inspire the counterpart, potentially leading to a favorable resolution.

7.5. Applying Social Skills in Negotiation

Social skills involve both verbal and non-verbal communication. These include active listening, expressing yourself clearly, and accurately reading your counterpart's cues to understand their perspective better.

Exceptional social skills mean you can adjust and fine-tune your style to resonate with your counterpart. This helps build rapport, trust, and ultimately, positive and productive relationships.

7.6. Conclusion

Emotional Intelligence is a sophisticated toolkit for success in any negotiation setting. It equips you to understand, interact, and influence others productively whilst ensuring composure and resilience in the face of adversity.

By leveraging emotional intelligence and fostering these crucial skills, you can transform your negotiation style and improve outcomes universally. Not only in your professional life but also in your personal interactions every day. Remember, mastering negotiation skills isn't about winning or losing; it's about forging alliances, fostering cooperation, and building relationships that benefit everyone involved. You're not just gaining a skill; you're transforming your life.

Chapter 8. Crafting and Delivering Compelling Messages

Compelling messages can serve as powerful tools to express our thoughts and intentions effectively. They capture attention, elegantly convey information and inspire responsiveness. These messages become a bridge of understanding between you and your audience. Let's unlock the methods to craft and deliver them with effectiveness.

8.1. Understanding the Art of Crafting Messages

Creating powerful messages isn't just about stringing together some fancy words; it involves understanding the audience, their needs, and their perspectives. Here are some insights into how one can master this art:

1. **Know your audience:** Before you can create an engaging message, you must first understand who you're speaking with. Determine their interests, needs, fears, dreams or challenges. As you tailor a message that resonates with your audience, it becomes influential.

2. **Focus on clarity:** Communication relies on clarity. Cluttered messages filled with industry jargon or unnecessary details can confuse the listener. Be succinct, precise, and transparent in your language to avoid any confusion.

3. **Create emotional connections:** Humans are emotional beings. Craft your message to tap into these emotions to make the conversation meaningful. Whether it's excitement, fear, anticipation or joy– if your audience feels a connection, they'll be

more attentive.

4. **Convey the benefits:** The audience is likely to be more interested if they perceive a direct benefit from your communication. Make sure your message includes how it will add value to their lives.

8.2. The Power of Storytelling

Storytelling is a time-tested technique of effective communication that encompasses all the elements mentioned above - understanding, clarity, emotional connection, and benefits. It personalizes information, making it more relatable and therefore memorable.

1. **Relatable Characters:** Characters are the heart of any story. A relatable character makes a story engaging and meaningful. Always try to build a character your audience can connect with.

2. **Fact-Infused Fiction:** A good story is not always about fantasy. A fact-infused story retains the appeal of a tale while also relaying critical information.

3. **The Emotional Arc:** A story with a strong emotional arc is more memorable. The ups and downs in the narrative make the story more immersive and create intrigue for the audience.

8.3. Framework for Delivering Compelling Messages

After crafting a compelling message, it's time to focus on delivery. Your style of delivery can amplify the impact of your message or dilute it.

1. **Confidence:** Whether speaking to a single person or presenting to a large audience, exuding confidence in your delivery is crucial. Build your knowledge base, rehearse your message, control your pace, and maintain eye contact to come across as

confident.

2. **Voice modulation:** The tone of your voice can uplift or depress your message's energy. Modulate your voice to express emotions adequately and stress on crucial points.

3. **Body Language:** Non-verbal cues form a major part of communication. Ensure that your body language aligns well with the message that you're trying to convey.

4. **Responsive Listening:** Communication isn't just about talking; it's about listening as well. Pay heed to your audience's reactions during the conversation. Adjust your communication based on these cues to ensure your message resonates.

8.4. The Power of Repetition

Repetition can strengthen the impact of your message, making it more memorable. However, it's essential that repetition is done subtly and tastefully, without making the message monotonous. Some practical ways you can use repetition are:

1. **Reiterate Key Points:** Echo the main points of your message at regular intervals during your speech or conversation.

2. **Use Analogies:** Analogies are great tools to repeat a point in different ways.

3. **Incorporate Visual Aids:** Use visuals repeatedly to anchor your message deeper into the minds of your audience.

Compelling messages are an art form that requires both practice and understanding. As you craft your thoughts skillfully and deliver them with authenticity, you will cultivate a more dynamic communication style. This will elevate your connections, inspire your audience, and catalyze your ambitions. Be persistent, be patient, and watch the transformative power of compelling messaging unfold.

Chapter 9. Overcoming Communication Barriers and Misunderstandings

Effective communicators not only speak and write well but also listen attentively, responding thoughtfully to the message conveyed. It's an ongoing process marked by continuous learning and refinement. Yet, it's all too common to encounter obstacles in the communication process. These hurdles, known as 'communication barriers', can lead to misunderstandings, stalled projects, and strained relationships. This chapter outlines several well-understood barriers, proposes means to overcome them, and includes strategies to prevent future miscommunication.

9.1. Types of Communication Barriers

Communication barriers can manifest in many forms. By understanding them, we're already halfway to solving the problem.

9.1.1. Physical Barriers

Physical barriers include tangible elements that can impede or prevent communication, such as noisy environments, a malfunctioned communication device, or physical distance between interlocutors. To overcome these, consider utilizing noise cancellation technology, regular equipment health checks, or leveraging remote collaboration tools that bridge the distance gap.

9.1.2. Psychological Barriers

Anxiety, stress, and emotional turmoil can block effective communication. To manage this, practice mindfulness and emotional intelligence, focusing on self-awareness and emotional regulation.

9.1.3. Semantic Barriers

The same words can mean different things to different people due to variations in background, experiences, and culture. Ensuring clarity upfront by defining terms or using simple language helps address this.

9.1.4. Process Barriers

This is about how communication is structured in organizations, such as hierarchy and rigid procedures, which might stifle free expression. You can tackle this barrier by promoting a culture of open dialogue and transparent feedback loops.

9.2. Overcoming Misunderstandings

Misunderstandings often occur when messages are unclear, misinterpreted, or ignored. Here are a few strategies to help you sail through these murky waters.

9.2.1. Seek Clarity

In the face of confusion, never hesitate to seek clarity. Ask questions. Pursue specifics. It's better to spend slightly more time understanding than moving forward on assumptions and risking errors.

9.2.2. Give and Request Feedback

Communication should be a two-way process, involving both sending and receiving information. Regularly checking for understanding helps ensure your message is received as intended.

9.2.3. Practice Active Listening

Active listening involves fully concentrating, understanding, responding, and then remembering what is being said. It validates the speaker and shows a genuine interest in their ideas.

9.3. Enhancing Your Communication Skills

Now that we've tackled barriers and misunderstandings, let's focus on the crucial skills you can develop to avoid them from cropping up.

9.3.1. Articulation and Clarity

Being articulate involves speaking or writing in a manner that's clear, fluent, and coherent. It's about transmitting your message in straightforward terms and cutting through jargon.

9.3.2. Non-Verbal Cues

Understanding and effectively using non-verbal cues like eye contact, facial expressions, and body language can greatly reduce misunderstanding and strengthen the effectiveness of our communication.

9.3.3. Empathy in Communication

By stepping into another's shoes and understanding their

perspective, we foster better communication. Empathy creates a safe platform for open dialogue and encourages problem-solving conversations.

9.3.4. Cultural Competency

If you're communicating with people from various cultures, it's vital to understand and respect their traditions, values, and communication styles. Being aware of cultural nuances helps overcome potential barriers, promoting seamless and respectful interaction.

Effective communication is an art, but it's also a science with defined steps and strategies. Overcoming barriers and preventing misunderstandings are critical aspects of mastering this craft. By enhancing your skills and employing proactive measures, you will unlock the full potential of your communication capabilities, enriching not only your professional relationships but also your personal ones. With every conversation, you'll be learning and growing, embodying the principles of effective communication, and moving closer to becoming a master communicator.

Chapter 10. Mastering the Power of Persuasion in Leadership

Persuasion has been an effective tool in the hands of leaders for centuries, molding the course of history. Emperors and generals, politicians and activists - across the spectrum, the ability to persuade has set apart the great leaders from the good. Understanding and mastering the art of persuasion enhances your leadership skills, making you more effective in engaging, motivating, and influencing your team, stakeholders, and even opponents.

10.1. Understanding Persuasion

Persuasion is the ability to convince others to accept your viewpoint or follow your direction. It isn't about exercising authority or highlighting the hierarchical structure; rather, it's about fostering a sense of shared understanding and mutual benefit. Strong persuasion skills come from a deep understanding of human psychology and the dynamics of communication.

To begin with, let's explore the three fundamental pillars of persuasion defined by the classical Greek philosopher, Aristotle - ethos, pathos, and logos.

Ethos refers to the credibility or trustworthiness of the speaker. Your team or audience are more likely to be influenced when you establish your credibility effectively. A good reputation, expertise, and transparency are typical factors that contribute to ethos.

Pathos denotes the emotional connection you can establish with your audience. Stirring emotions can help your message resonate better. Sharing relatable stories, experiences or appealing to shared values can create this emotional bond.

Logos revolves around the logic and reasoning behind your argument. Your audience must understand and agree with your logic before they can be persuaded. Therefore, ensure that your argument is well-structured, thorough, and supported with compelling evidence.

Incorporating these three pillars in your interaction enhances your persuasive potency. As a leader, your main responsibility is not just to communicate, but also to convince and inspire. The utilization of ethos, pathos, and logos makes this possible.

10.2. Constructing a Persuasive Argument

The construction of your persuasive argument must be deliberate and strategic. Your argument can be considered as a well-crafted piece of architecture, wherein each element plays a crucial role in delivering a persuasive message. Here's how you can construct a persuasive argument.

Start with a clear, concise statement of your position or what you desire. This acts as the foundation of your argument and sets the tone for the discussion.

Then present your evidence, which supports your position. Your evidence must be credible, relevant, and preferably from multiple sources. Also, make sure to offer an interpretation of the evidence, connecting it back to your main argument.

Next, engage with opposing viewpoints or potential objections. This signals respect for your audience and demonstrates your thorough understanding of the subject. Address the objections convincingly, using your evidence and logic to dismantle the opposing arguments.

Conclude with a strong appeal to your audience, summarizing your position and inviting them to align with your perspective. Your conclusion should offer an actionable directive that your audience can take, which aligns with your argument.

10.3. Emotional Intelligence and Persuasion

Emotional intelligence (EI) is a powerful tool in persuasive communication. EI is the intersection of emotions and intelligence - your ability to recognize, understand, and manage your own emotions and those of others.

The recognition and understanding of emotions allow you to gauge the mood of your team, adapt your communication accordingly, and respond to their reactions effectively. By managing your emotions, you can maintain a calm demeanour, even in challenging situations.

As a leader, you often need to inspire and motivate your team. With EI, you can tailor your message to resonate emotionally with your team, thereby igniting their inner motivation.

10.4. Framing and Reframing: The Power of Perception

How you frame your arguments can significantly influence the persuasiveness of your speech.

Framing involves presenting your argument in a certain light or from a specific perspective. It leverages cognitive biases, and guides the audience's perception and interpretation of your message.

Positive framing, focusing on the benefits or gains, tends to be useful when you want to encourage proactive behavior or decisions. On the other hand, negative framing, emphasizing potential losses or negative consequences, can be effective in discouraging certain actions or promoting risk aversion.

Reframing is a response tool used when a counter-argument is presented. Instead of directly opposing it, you reframe the issue in a new light or from a different perspective, thereby effecting a subtle shift in perception.

10.5. Storytelling in Persuasive Leadership

As humans, we are natural storytellers and responders to stories. Therefore, incorporating narratives into your persuasive arguments appeals to the human affinity for stories.

Leadership stories can convey vision, values, and strategies. They can help bridge the gap between management and employees, fostering a sense of unity and shared purpose. Use stories to highlight successes, lessons learned from failures, and to share the common values that bind the team.

In conclusion, mastering the power of persuasion is an essential aspect of leadership. It involves understanding the psychology and dynamics of communication, constructing persuasive arguments, leveraging emotional intelligence, effective framing of issues, and storytelling. As you advance in your leadership journey, these techniques will empower you to motivate your team, influence stakeholders, and overcome resistance effectively. Embrace this art and constantly refine your skills, and witness a transformation in your leadership style and outcomes.

Chapter 11. Harnessing Persuasion Power: Real-World Applications

Understanding the intricacies of power in persuasion involves an exploration of various dimensions - from negotiation strategies, social influence, and charisma, to non-verbal communication and storytelling skills. As you venture through this chapter, you'll unlock the elements that when knitted together, create a powerfully persuasive communicator. More importantly, we'll delve into myriad real-world examples, drawing lessons from both successful escapades and disastrous gaffes alike.

11.1. Understanding Persuasion and Power

Persuasion is a complex, multifaceted art, strongly rooted in understanding human psychology. Effective persuasion has a symbiotic relationship with power; it harnesses power to make arguments compelling, and in turn, a proficient persuader holds significant influence over others.

In essence, persuasion is the process of causing someone's attitude, belief, or behavior to change through arguments, reasoning, or symbolism. These tactics, however, derive their power from a variety of sources including the persuader's credibility, the emotional resonance of the message, or the logical strength of the argument, among other things.

In this context, power is the capacity to cause change. It influences the capacity and reputation to make things happen. It's often seen as position or title, but in reality, it extends beyond mere authority and includes personal traits like charisma, reputation, expertise, and connections.

Before delving into practical strategies, let's analyze a real-world instance. Consider the way Apple markets its products. The company frequently uses phrases like "the best iPhone ever" or "the most powerful iPad." While quite bold, the words tap into our desire for owning impressive tech. Coupled with Apple's authority and history of innovation, the persuasive message turns into a compelling proposition, highlighting the undefined but real power of persuasion.

11.2. Negotiation Strategies: Power Moves

In the world of business, negotiation is a persuasive art that directly affects corporate success. Whether you are negotiating a multimillion-dollar contract or seeking a small concession from a colleague, you'll rely on persuasion power.

Understanding the negotiation process technically and psychologically is essential for successful outcomes. Preparation is key. Clarify your goals, research your counterparts, and develop an understanding of what is negotiable. Remember, negotiations are the conversations that lead to agreement.

Consider the example of Herb Cohen, a renowned negotiator who has worked with international conflicts, hostage negotiations, and business deals. His motto, "Power is based upon perception — if you think you've got it then you've got it," encapsulates the essence of the negotiation game. He leverages persuasion skills, understanding his counterpart's perspective and presenting arguments in a way that appeals to them.

Chapter 12. Storytelling: An Ingenious Tool

Storytelling is perhaps the most potent tool for persuasion. Narratives add a human touch to messages; they appeal to our emotions and are easier to remember. When stories are well-told, they have the power to change our opinion, inspire action, or create a lasting impact.

The power of stories isn't confined to social settings or marketing campaigns; it's widely used in politics as well. Politicians like Barack Obama and Ronald Reagan leveraged the power of storytelling to create emotional connections with their audience, making their political messages more compelling.

Consider the example of Malala Yousafzai's compelling UN speech in 2013. She shared her story of battling against the Taliban for girls' education. Her storytelling strength, combined with her credible experience, stirred the global community, influencing policy changes and philanthropic actions. As she so remarkably attests, "One child, one teacher, one book, one pen, can change the world."

12.1. The Power of Non-Verbal Communication

Non-verbal cues, including body language, facial expressions, and tone of voice, constitute a substantial part of our communication. In fact, studies suggest that around 93% of all communication is non-verbal.

Considering a real-world scenario, imagine you're having a conversation with a colleague who's saying "fine" but maintains a crossed posture and a tense facial expression. Even though the words suggest agreement, the non-verbal cues contradict, leading you to question the honesty behind the response.

Non-verbal communication significantly influences the outcomes of job interviews, business negotiations, and public speaking. Body language is a powerful tool in manifesting confidence and building rapport. Mastering non-verbal communication enhances your ability to persuade others subtly but effectively.

Practice maintaining eye contact, using open body language, and modulating your voice. Learn to read others' non-verbal cues to understand their reactions better. Successful leaders like Tony Robbins often emphasize the importance of body language in effective communication, asserting how powerful gestures and body postures can add a punch to a persuasive message.

12.2. Persuasion Ethics: The Line of Power

While discussing persuasion's power, it's important to address the ethical dimension. Power can be misused, and persuasive communication can slip into manipulation territory, causing harm or leading people to act against their best interests.

Consider the unfortunate example of the Fyre Festival fiasco. Marketed as an ultra-luxurious music event with persuasive advertisements featuring influential celebrities, it turned out to be a disaster. Stranded attendees found poor conditions instead of the promised luxury, proving that the persuaders had wielded the weapon of persuasion unethically.

Keep in mind that, while persuasion holds immense potential for facilitating positive outcomes, overstepping ethical boundaries poses severe risks. Strong persuasion combined with sincere intentions and respect for the other party ensures long-term positive relationships and successful communication.

Harnessing the power of your persuasion involves understanding human psychology, practicing negotiation, wielding the weapon of storytelling, mastering non-verbal communication, and adhering to ethical guidelines. As you walk through this journey of mastering persuasion, you'll rewrite your narrative, transforming from an effective communicator into a true influencer.

Remember, persuasive communication is an art that you cultivate over time through practice and patience. With each interaction, you have the opportunity to refine your approach and improve your impact. The true power of persuasion lies not just in winning arguments or sealing deals, but in making heartening connections, moving ideas forward, and weaving a network of positive influence.

And in the end, isn't that what true power is all about?